TOUCHDOWN

THE POWER AND PRECISION OF FOOTBALL'S PERFECT PLAY

MARK STEWART AND MIKE KENNEDY

Ⓜ Millbrook Press • Minneapolis

The following image were provided by the Authors: Harper's Weekly, p. 9; Team Stewart, p. 10; Murad Tobacco, pp. 11, 13; Street & Smith Publishers, p. 12; Collegiate Collection, p. 17 (top); National Chicle, p. 17 (bottom); Topps, Inc., pp. 19 (top), 21 (bottom), 23 (bottom), 25 (both), 27 (bottom), 29 (top); Phila. Chewing Gum Corp., p. 19 (bottom); TCMA, Ltd., p. 21 (top); Empire Press, p. 23 (top); The Peterson Companies, p. 27 (top); NFL Pro Set, p. 29 (bottom); The Upper Deck Company, LLC, pp. 31 (top), 33 (bottom); Black Book Partners, pp. 31 (bottom), 41; Fleer/Sky Box International LP., p. 33 (top); SAGE*HIT, p. 35 (top); Press Pass, Inc., p. 35 (bottom); National Football League, p. 38.

The following images are used with the permission of: © Otto Greule Jr./Getty Images, pp. 4, 60 (top); © NFL/NFL/Getty Images, pp. 6, 24, 53, 56, 59 (top); © Scott Boehm/Getty Images, p. 14; © Hulton Archive/Getty Images, p. 16; © Pro Football Hall of Fame/NFL/Getty Images, pp. 18, 20, 22; © Bruce Bennett Studios/Getty Images, p. 26; © Al Messerschmidt/Al Messerschmidt Archive/Getty Images, pp. 28, 44, 50; © Boston College/Collegiate Images/Getty Images, p. 30; © Allen Kee/NFL/Getty Images, p. 32; © Donald Miralle/Getty Images, p. 34; © New York Times Co./Hulton Archive/Getty Images, p. 37; © Darryl Norenberg/NFL/Getty Images, pp. 39, 40; © Bruce Dierdorff/NFL/Getty Images, p. 42; © Mark Leffingwell/AFP/Getty Images, p. 43; © Brian Bahr/Getty Images, p. 45; © Joe Robbins/Getty Images, pp. 46, 58 (top); © Win McNamee/Getty Images, p. 47; © Edwin Mahan/NFL/Getty Images, p. 49; © Steve Grayson/WireImage/Getty Images, p. 54; © Doug Pensinger/Getty Images, p. 55; © George Long/NFL/Getty Images, p. 57; © Focus on Sport/Getty Images, p. 58 (bottom); © Al Pereira/Getty Images, p. 59 (bottom); © Al Bello/Getty Images, p. 60 (bottom); © Lisa Blumenfeld/Getty Images, p. 62.

Front Cover: © Jim Rogash/NFL/Getty Images.
Front Cover Flap: © Steve Grayson/WireImage/Getty Images (left); © Otto Greule Jr./Getty Images (right).

Unless otherwise indicated, the memorabilia photographed in this book is from the collection of the authors. The logos and registered trademarks pictured are the property of the teams, leagues, and companies listed above. The authors are not affiliated with any of these organizations.

Millbrook Press
A division of Lerner Publishing Group, Inc.
241 First Avenue North
Minneapolis, MN 55401 U.S.A.

Website address: www.lernerbooks.com

Library of Congress Cataloging-in-Publication Data

Stewart, Mark, 1960–
        Touchdown : the power and precision of football's perfect play / by Mark Stewart and Mike Kennedy.
            p.   cm.
        Includes index.
        ISBN: 978–0–8225–8751–4 (lib. bdg. : alk. paper)
        1. Football—Juvenile literature. I. Kennedy, Mike (Mike William), 1965– II. Title.
    GV950.7.S66 2010
    796.33—dc22   2008044295

Manufactured in the United States of America
2 – DP – 7/1/10

CONTENTS

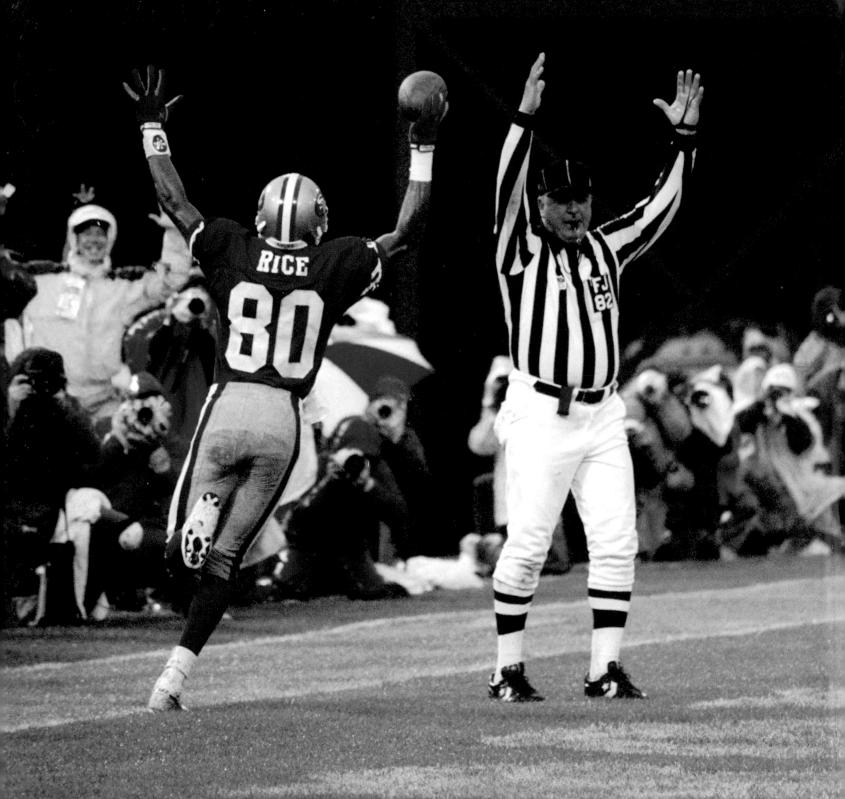

INTRODUCTION

One of the most thrilling plays in sports is the touchdown. Few moments combine such power and emotion. Scoring a touchdown is a reason for wild celebration. Allowing a touchdown is a terrible feeling.

Whenever a player reaches the end zone, it is usually the result of a great individual effort and tremendous teamwork. Hour after hour, football teams practice ways to score touchdowns. At the same time, they work just as hard learning how to stop touchdowns.

A look inside a football playbook can tell you a lot about touchdowns. On every play, everyone on the field has a job to do. If everything goes exactly as planned, the player with the ball has a chance to score. This is when football's superstars get their chance to shine.

Where did the touchdown come from? How many different ways can a team score a touchdown? Which players specialized in scoring touchdowns? Who holds the most amazing touchdown records? Who will break those records in the future? This book not only answers these questions—it looks at the touchdown in interesting ways you may never have considered.

Jerry Rice celebrates one of the 197 scoring catches he made during his career. Two arms raised to the sky is the official signal for a touchdown.

DISTANT REPLAY 1

THE HISTORY OF THE TOUCHDOWN

Who scored the first touchdown? The history books tell the story of a young man named William Webb Ellis. He was a student at the Rugby School in Great Britain in 1823. A favorite of the Rugby boys was a game called football. It was a rough game that had been played in England for many centuries.

Foot-ball was similar to soccer, with two important differences. First, a player was allowed to catch a long kick, set it down, and then boot it the other way. A point was awarded to a team that kicked the ball over the goal line. Second, there was not a fixed goal—with posts, a crossbar and a net—as there is in modern soccer.

All games at the Rugby School ended precisely at five in the evening. One day, as young William prepared to catch a long kick, the school's bell began chiming out five gongs. He knew he didn't have enough time to score a goal in the traditional way. So William plucked the ball out of the air, put his head down, and ran right through his stunned opponents. He crossed the goal line and touched the ball to the ground before the final gong had sounded.

William's classmates argued whether his play should count. Some said yes, and others said no. Almost all agreed, however, that William's unexpected play might

A ballcarrier dives forward during a 1915 game between the Canton Bulldogs and Columbus Panhandles. A century earlier, this would have been a very odd sight. Back then, carrying the ball was against the rules.

7

make for a fine new game. If a player was allowed to carry the ball, then it only seemed fair that his opponents should be allowed to pull him to the ground. And since the ballcarrier had little chance of outrunning an entire team, shouldn't his teammates be allowed to protect him? These rules formed the foundation of tackling and blocking.

The old game of foot-ball soon became two new sports. The "kicking game" turned into what we know as soccer. (Outside of the United States and Canada it is still called football.) The "carrying game" was called rugby, after the school where it started. In North America, a third game developed that was a little bit of both. Some called it American football.

American football was played mostly in boarding schools and universities. During the 1800s, travel could be very difficult and expensive. School teams did not play against one another as they do now. As a result, each school made up its own rules for football. At some schools, it was a very violent sport. At others, penalties were given for rough play.

Two schools in New Jersey played by very similar rules. Princeton University and Rutgers University were only a few miles apart. For many years, their students had competed over an enormous cannon left over from the American Revolution (1775–1783). The strongest boys from Princeton would sneak onto the Rutgers campus and steal the cannon. The strongest boys from Rutgers would then steal it back. Many injuries occurred during these pranks. Princeton stopped this dangerous game by sinking the cannon into concrete. Looking for a new way to compete, the boys decided to hold a football contest. On November 6, 1869, the first football game took place between two colleges.

A modern football fan would barely recognize the Princeton–Rutgers game. There were twenty-five players to a side on the field at the same time. A point could be scored only by kicking the ball—which was round—between two posts at either end of the field. A team moved the ball forward by dribbling it with the feet. A player was

Harvard and Columbia play a game of football in the 1870s. The sport was only a few years old at the time.

not allowed to carry the ball. However, a wall of blockers was able to protect the dribbler. When a team could no longer move the ball forward, it had to kick to the other team.

Rutgers beat Princeton in that first game 6–4. Two weeks later, the schools played again. Princeton won this time 8–0. There were no touchdowns, only one-point goals.

Other North American colleges soon began playing football. The sport grew in popularity. In 1874 the football teams from McGill University in Montreal, Canada, and Harvard University in Cambridge, Massachusetts, squared off for two games. The games were played with an egg-shaped rugby ball.

The first game was played by McGill's rules. The second was played by Harvard's rules. Harvard was known for its slow, rugged playing style. McGill favored a faster game that was very close to British rugby. This made sense, because Canada was part of the British Empire at the time.

The Harvard players liked McGill's style. They enjoyed running with the football. They were also amazed how straight the oddly shaped ball flew when it was kicked. The play they liked most of all was when a runner crossed the goal line and triumphantly touched the ball down on the ground. The McGill players called it a touchdown. Thanks to this meeting, more than a century later, American football and Canadian football are almost identical games. Canadian football is played on a slightly larger field, and a team has three tries instead of four to make a first down. Many football stars from U.S. high schools and colleges end up playing in the Canadian Football League.

Walter Camp

In 1876 captains from several U.S. universities met to form the Intercollegiate Football Association. They agreed on a set of rules everyone could follow. A touchdown was worth 1 point. A goal kicked from the field was worth 4 points. This is the origin of the term *field goal*.

These rules meant that a player running toward the goal line would score more points by stopping and kicking the ball instead of continuing forward. Imagine a running back such as Adrian Peterson sprinting for the end zone—and then stopping short to boot the ball between the goalposts!

During the next few years, the value of a touchdown changed. So did the sport of football itself. For a time, a touchdown did not count for any points—it simply gave the scoring team a free kick in front of the goal. This probably was the origin of the extra point. Today teams that score touchdowns get a free kick from a few yards away, which is worth 1 point. They can also try to carry the ball into the end zone for 2 points.

During the 1880s, more rules were added. Football started to look a little more like the modern game. A coach at Yale University named Walter Camp introduced many of football's innovations. Camp is considered by many to be the father of football.

By the end of the 1800s, however, football still had a way to go. Most games were decided by brute force instead of exciting scoring plays. Ballcarriers worked their way down the field behind a wall of blockers. The blockers linked their arms and formed a V-shaped wedge. They trampled anyone who tried to run through them. Another popular play was known as the turtleback. The ballcarrier stayed inside a round "shell" of blockers that moved slowly down the field. The only way to make a tackle was to jump over the shell or try to crash through it. Hundreds of players suffered serious injuries each season, and a few even died while playing football.

By the turn of the century, many colleges thought football was too violent. They shut down their teams. President Theodore Roosevelt had played and loved football as a student at Harvard. Even so, in 1905, he threatened to ban the sport. The top schools held a meeting to discuss the future of football. The most dangerous plays were outlawed. The number of yards needed to make a first down (and keep the football) was doubled, from 5 to 10. This forced a team to "open up" its offense and spread out its players.

Another rule that was changed drew almost no attention. Before 1905, if a player threw the football through the air, it had to travel backward. This was one of the main rules of rugby. But in 1905, the forward pass became legal.

During the next thirty years, modern football began to take shape. Kicking was still an important part of the game. However, now a team could put points on the board in many different ways. Plays were invented to get a fast runner into the open field and across the goal line. Passing became more popular. Even though

As this trading card shows, kicking was a much more important part of football in the early 1900s than it is today.

throwing the ball was risky, more and more games were being won with thrilling touchdown passes. There were more punts in the early 1900s than there are in modern football. That meant there were more daring punt returns. Nothing brought fans to their feet like a punt returned the length of the field for a touchdown.

The biggest change in the game was how fans began viewing the best players. In the old days, football players were seen as brutes. They relied on brawn rather than brains. They were often covered in mud. Their sport was very dangerous, and they

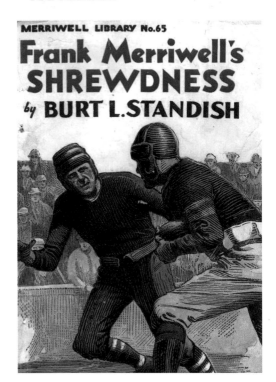

MERRIWELL LIBRARY No.65

Frank Merriwell's
SHREWDNESS
by BURT L.STANDISH

Frank Merriwell was a make-believe hero of children's books in the early 1900s. When college football became popular, Frank suited up for his school and became a star.

risked life and limb for their schools and universities. Now football players were dashing, heroic figures. They were the "big men on campus." Children dreamed of following in their footsteps.

By the 1920s, kids' books were being written about football players. This would have been unthinkable a few years earlier. By the 1930s, football was second only to baseball as the country's favorite sport. The touchdown maker was now a star!

Meanwhile, a race was starting between the offense and the defense. Every time someone thought up a new way to score a touchdown, the defense would have to find a way to prevent that play from working. This competition was waged by the players on the field and also by the coaches on the sidelines. Coaches stood in front of chalkboards for hours, marking out Xs and Os. They hoped to discover the next great play—or at least how to stop the great plays of their opponents.

For the last seventy-five years or so, teams have featured two basic strategies for scoring touchdowns. In the first, a team tries to gain small amounts of yardage using the power and quickness of its blockers. The goal is to wear down the opponent's defense and eventually carry the ball into the end zone.

In the second strategy, a team tries to create running room for its fastest player. Once a running back or receiver has the ball in the open field, he has a good chance of outrunning or outmaneuvering the defensive players. Teams get the ball to their best players with a well-designed pass or a perfectly designed run. Over the years, most teams have found clever ways to combine these two strategies. It gives them the element of surprise. Will a team try a pass or a run? No one knows until the play starts.

SAFETY FIRST

The basics of football have changed little over the past one hundred years. But the equipment that players wear has come a very long way. Indeed, modern touchdown makers would feel "naked" wearing helmets and pads from the early days of football.

The first football helmets were little more than leather caps. They prevented scrapes and cuts but did not absorb much energy during hard blows to the head. Early helmets did not have face masks, either. Some players, however, chose to wear a nose guard (*below*). It is also worth noting that the sport was played differently. Runners did not use their heads as "battering rams" the way they do now. Tacklers did not drive their helmets into blockers and ballcarriers.

Hard plastic helmets did not arrive until the late 1940s. Many advances in plastics and polymers were made during World War II (1939–1945). These improvements found their way into football in the 1950s. Hard helmets were not only safer—they were also strong enough to hold a face mask in place.

Plastic also made shoulder pads lighter and stronger. Old-time players wore pads made of leather and cardboard. This type of padding did not offer much protection. With more effective shoulder pads, players could use their upper bodies to crash into one another. New types of rubber also helped, making padding softer and better at absorbing energy.

New equipment had a big effect on football in the 1950s and 1960s. Players felt better protected, so the game got faster and the hitting got harder. Fans loved it. The popularity of football—particularly the pro game—grew very quickly. The new equipment also kept the best players from getting worn out. Careers lasted longer. The top stars could play for ten years or more if they avoided major injury. This made it even more fun for fans to follow their favorite teams.

Over the past thirty or forty years, football equipment has continued to improve. The most important changes are in helmets. They are carefully designed to prevent brain injuries such as concussions. Various energy-absorbing materials are used, often in several layers. Football will always be a dangerous game, but in many ways, it is safer than ever.

Which touchdowns are the most fun to watch? That really depends upon the fan watching from the stands or at home on television. Some fans like to see a rough, tough player burst across the goal line—where every inch is important. Some prefer a dodging, twirling run for the end zone—when a player seems as if he is walking a tightrope. Others stand and cheer for the 50-yard footrace in the open field—where the ballcarrier tries to speed by the fastest defender.

With quarterbacks throwing the ball more than ever, the passing touchdown has also become very popular. On a perfectly timed pass play, the ball and receiver arrive in the same spot at the same time. From there, the receiver is on his own.

Sometimes the pass is not on target. The receiver must leap, dive, or twist in midair to catch the ball. Some of football's greatest touchdowns have been scored this way.

A touchdown can be the result of a long drive to the goal line. It can also be a single and sudden breathtaking play. Either way, the result is the same: six points on the scoreboard and thousands of cheering fans.

Santonio Holmes stretches for the game-winning touchdown in Super Bowl XLIII. His amazing catch was the perfect ending to an exciting game.

BREAKING THE PLANE 2

TEN UNFORGETTABLE TOUCHDOWNS

When a runner smashes his way toward a touchdown, the referees try to position themselves so they can look down the goal line. When the ballcarrier is tackled right at the line, they must decide whether the ball has "broken the plane"—or crossed the imaginary barrier between the playing field and the end zone. If it has, the referees raise both arms to signal a touchdown. When twenty-two players pile up, this is not an easy call to make!

Football experts are often asked to make an even harder call. They must look at the many thousands of touchdowns scored and decide which are the greatest ones. All touchdowns are not created equal. Some are much more important than others. Some win championships. Others break records. A touchdown can also alter the course of history. It can turn a substitute into a star. It can even change how the game is played.

Choosing football's greatest touchdowns can be a lot of fun—and a great way to start an argument. The following pages look at ten unforgettable scoring plays... read on and see if you agree!

NOTRE DAME USES A SECRET WEAPON AGAINST ARMY

NOVEMBER 1, 1913 • WEST POINT, NEW YORK

When Army (the U.S. Military Academy) agreed to host a game against Notre Dame University in 1913, most football fans thought the contest would be an easy "tune-up" for the Cadets. Army expected to win easily. Their most important game was a week later, against Navy (the U.S. Naval Academy). Notre Dame had a different idea.

Knute Rocke poses for a picture in 1925, after he had become Notre Dame's football coach.

Quarterback Gus Dorais and end Knute Rockne had been planning for the Army game for a long time. The two friends had spent the summer working at Cedar Point Resort in Sandusky, Ohio. In their spare time, they practiced hour after hour on a new play: the forward pass. Passing had been legal for some time, but most coaches believed it was too risky. The football at the time was much fatter than the modern ball. Players had difficulty throwing and catching it. However, Dorais and Rockne had mastered this art.

Army had stronger players than Notre Dame had. But strength was of no use against the speedy Rockne. He raced past the bulky Cadets to catch Dorais's passes. Notre Dame took a 14–13 halftime lead.

Things got worse for Army in the second half. No matter what the Cadets tried, Dorais found a way to throw the ball to Rockne. The Fighting Irish raced to a 35–13 victory. With its surprising win, Notre Dame told the football world that it was a school on the rise. More important, the sport was changed forever. Coaches, players, and fans across the nation realized the forward pass was a valuable weapon. It was here to stay.

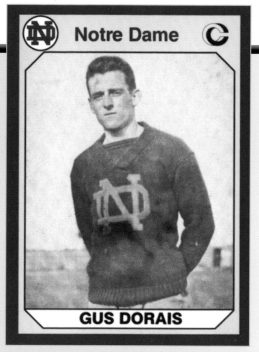

Notre Dame

GUS DORAIS

COLLECTOR'S CORNER

GUS DORAIS

Dorais was a senior for Notre Dame in 1913. He finished the game against Army with 14 completions in 17 attempts for 243 yards. Dorais would go on to win All-America honors that season.

1990 Collegiate Collection Gus Dorais card

KNUTE ROCKNE

One of the passes Rockne caught against Army went for 40 yards. The play set a new record in college football. Rockne later became the coach for Notre Dame and was one of the most famous sports figures in the United States.

1934 National Chicle Knute Rockne card

KNUTE ROCKNE

CHICAGO'S TRICK PLAY FOOLS THE GIANTS

DECEMBER 17, 1933 • CHICAGO, ILLINOIS

In the early days of the National Football League (NFL), college football was still king. NFL teams welcomed many former college stars. However, sports fans weren't sold on the league. It would take more than thirty years for the NFL to catch up in popularity.

One of the most important steps in this journey came in 1933. That season the NFL divided its teams into an East Division and West Division. The first-place teams in each division would meet for the championship of professional football.

In 1933 the Chicago Bears won the West Division. The New York Giants won the East Division. The two teams met at Wrigley Field in Chicago for the first NFL championship game. More than twenty-five thousand fans jammed into the stadium. This was a huge crowd for the league at this time. The United States was suffering through the Great Depression (1929–1942). Most people could not afford a football ticket. Those who could afford one got their money's worth in Chicago that day.

The Bears kicked a pair of field goals to go ahead 6–0. The Giants responded with a 29-yard pass from Red Badgro to Harry Newman for a touchdown. After another field goal by Chicago, New York scored its second touchdown to take a 14–9 lead. The teams then traded touchdowns. The Giants led 21–16 late in the fourth quarter.

Bill Hewitt pitches the ball to Billy Karr for Chicago's winning touchdown in the 1933 NFL championship game.

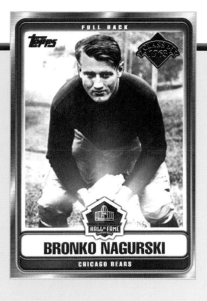

COLLECTOR'S CORNER

Bronko Nagurski

At 6'2" and 226 pounds, Nagurski was the most punishing runner of his time. It was his arm, however, that helped the Bears beat the Giants for the 1933 NFL title. He threw two touchdown passes in the game. Nagurski later became a world champion wrestler.

2006 Topps Bronko Nagurski card

Bill Hewitt

Hewitt was named All-NFL four times. He was known for making up trick plays, including the one that won the 1933 NFL championship for the Bears. Hewitt was one of the last players in the league who chose not to wear a helmet.

1988 Swell Bill Hewitt card

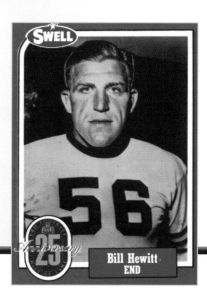

Chicago got the ball with only a few minutes remaining. The fans were on the edge of their seats. The Bears moved into New York territory. They put the ball in the hands of their fullback, Bronko Nagurski. He threw a pass downfield to Bill Hewitt. Before the Giants could tackle Hewitt, he flipped the ball to Billy Karr. Karr ran the rest of the way for the winning touchdown!

THE COLTS BEAT THE GIANTS IN SUDDEN DEATH

DECEMBER 28, 1958 • NEW YORK, NEW YORK

During the 1950s, the New York Giants were the most glamorous team in football. No club was more entertaining or had more star power. New York had a handsome halfback named Frank Gifford and a tough-as-nails quarterback named Charlie Conerly. In 1956 the Giants were champions of the NFL.

In 1958 the Giants looked as if they were headed for another championship. Standing in their way were the hard-nosed Baltimore Colts. Their top player was Johnny Unitas. He was a no-nonsense quarterback who was at his best when the pressure was on. The matchup between the glitzy Giants and the gritty Colts captured the imagination of football fans everywhere. Thanks to a deal made by NFL commissioner Bert Bell, the game would be televised across the nation.

The Giants kicked a field goal in the first quarter. The Colts took the lead with two touchdowns in the second quarter. New York went back ahead with a pair of touchdowns in the second half. The Giants held a 17–14 lead with time running out.

Baltimore got the ball back deep in its own territory. Unitas moved his team down the field. With less than ten seconds left, Steve Myhra kicked a field goal to tie the game.

Baltimore's Alan Ameche scores in overtime to beat the Giants in the "greatest game ever played."

In the past, a game tied after sixty minutes ended that way (with no winner). This would not do for a championship game. In 1955 the NFL had created a "sudden death" rule. The teams would play an overtime period. The first team to score would be the winner.

The Giants received the ball to start overtime. The Baltimore defense forced New York to punt. The Colts sensed their chance to win. Unitas marched his team to New York's 1-yard line. He then handed off to his fullback, Alan Ameche, who was nicknamed the Horse for this powerful running style. Ameche galloped into the end zone for the winning score. The Colts won 23–17 and were NFL champs. Many decades later, football fans still buzzed with excitement over the "greatest game ever played."

COLLECTOR'S CORNER

Johnny Unitas
Unitas was nicknamed Mr. Clutch for his coolness during the most tense moments of a game. In the game-tying drive against the Giants, he completed all seven of his passes.

1980 TCMA
Johnny Unitas
card

Alan Ameche
Ameche won the Heisman Trophy as the nation's top college football player in 1954. With the Colts, he was selected to play in the Pro Bowl (the NFL's All-Star Game) four times.

1956 Topps Alan Ameche card

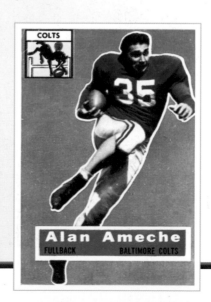

THE PACKERS PUT THE COWBOYS ON ICE

DECEMBER 31, 1967 • GREEN BAY, WISCONSIN

Coaches do not come any tougher than Vince Lombardi. He expected his players to be perfect. It did not matter who the opponent was or what the conditions were. Lombardi's Green Bay Packers joked that he treated them all equally—like dogs! Still, the Packers became a great team under Lombardi. They played with confidence and discipline.

The Packers prepared to meet the Dallas Cowboys for the NFL championship in 1967. They also prepared for the cold. No one could remember a chillier day for a title game. The thermometer read –13°F. The wind whipped off Lake Michigan and made the weather feel 30°F colder. Lombardi thought it was a perfect day for a football game!

The Packers charged to a 14–0 lead. But two Green Bay fumbles allowed the Cowboys to make a comeback. Lombardi was not happy with his team's mistakes. He became more frustrated after Dallas moved ahead 17–14 on a trick play. Running back Dan Reeves took a handoff and then threw a 50-yard touchdown pass to Lance Rentzel.

Down by three points with five

Bart Starr (#15) squeezes over the goal line for the winning touchdown in the "Ice Bowl."

SEPTEMBER 1987 U.S. $2.95, CAN. $3.50

SPORTS HISTORY

National League
Hits .303

Last Minute
NFL Championship

Sam Snead's
Quest

Knute Rockne
and Notre Dame
Lombardi Legacy

VINCE LOMBARDI

The 1967 season was Lombardi's last as coach of the Packers. In nine years with Green Bay, he had a record of 89–29 and won five NFL championships.

1987 Vince Lombardi *Sports History* cover

BART STARR

PACKERS

QUARTERBACK • N.F.C.

BART STARR

Starr was a calm, cool leader. He carried out Lombardi's plays perfectly. Against the Cowboys, he suggested the winning play to his coach. Starr was the MVP of the first two Super Bowls.

1971 Topps Bart Starr card

minutes left, Green Bay got the ball back on its 32-yard line. Quarterback Bart Starr guided the Packers down the field. With one minute left, Green Bay lined up on the Dallas 1-yard line. The Cowboys twice kept the Packers out of the end zone. The Packers had time for just one more try. Should they kick a field goal to tie the game or go for the winning touchdown?

Starr and Lombardi agreed on a play. The quarterback would keep the ball and try to power into the end zone. Linemen Jerry Kramer and Ken Bowman would have to create an opening wide enough for Starr. On the final play of the game, now known as the Ice Bowl, Starr found that sliver of daylight. He dove across the goal line for a 21–17 victory.

FRANCO HARRIS RESCUES THE STEELERS

DECEMBER 23, 1972 • PITTSBURGH, PENNSYLVANIA

For their first thirty-nine years in the NFL, the Pittsburgh Steelers were known for losing. By 1972, however, the Steelers were beginning to show signs of life. Pittsburgh head coach Chuck Noll formed a new team around a young and talented defense. Scoring on the Steelers had once been easy. Now it was a nightmare. On offense, Pittsburgh had two good building blocks in quarterback Terry Bradshaw and rookie running back Franco Harris.

The Steelers won eleven games during the 1972 season and made the playoffs. Pittsburgh's opponent in the first round was the Oakland Raiders. They were one of the toughest, meanest teams in football. As most fans expected, the game was a defensive battle. Neither team scored in the first half. In the third quarter, the Steelers managed to kick a field goal. Later, they booted another to make the score 6–0. The Raiders fought back to take a 7–6 lead.

Pittsburgh fans were in agony as the Steelers began their final drive. With twenty-two seconds remaining, Bradshaw faced a fourth down on his own 40-yard line. The game had come down to one final play.

Franco Harris looks to see who's chasing him after his "Immaculate Reception."

Bradshaw dropped back and scanned the field for an open teammate. With the Raiders bearing down on him, he fired a desperate pass to Frenchy Fuqua. Oakland's Jack Tatum was right there to break up the play. Everyone froze as the ball bounced away. Pittsburgh's season was over.

Or was it? Harris, who was running toward the fluttering football, plucked it out of the air before it touched the playing surface. He looked up and saw no one in front of him. He raced across the goal line for the winning touchdown!

NFL rules in 1972 said that a player could not catch a ball that had bounced off his teammate. The officials decided that Tatum had touched the ball last and that Harris's catch was "clean"—so clean, claimed Steeler fans, that it was immaculate! In fact, the catch became forever known as the Immaculate Reception.

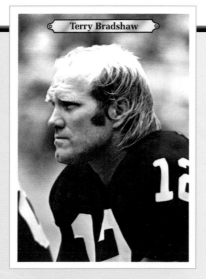

Terry Bradshaw

COLLECTOR'S CORNER

TERRY BRADSHAW
The Steelers did not make it to the Super Bowl in 1972, but Bradshaw would later lead them to four NFL titles. He was named the NFL's Most Valuable Player in 1978.

1980 Topps Super Terry Bradshaw card

FRANCO HARRIS
Harris was Pittsburgh's first pick in the 1972 NFL draft. In his rookie season, he rushed for more than 1,000 yards and 10 touchdowns.

1974 Topps Franco Harris card

FRANCO HARRIS RUNNING BACK
STEELERS

MONTANA AND CLARK CORRAL THE COWBOYS

JANUARY 10, 1982 • SAN FRANCISCO, CALIFORNIA

Dwight Clark leaps high for "the Catch" that beat the Cowboys.

During the 1970s, the Dallas Cowboys ruled the NFL's National Football Conference (NFC). As the top team in the NFC, Dallas had faced off against the winner of the NFL's other conference, the American Football Conference (AFC), in the Super Bowl five times during the decade. The Cowboys had won the big game twice. Their head coach, Tom Landry, helped talented players such as Roger Staubach, Tony Dorsett, Randy White, and Harvey Martin become stars.

In San Francisco, the 49ers were trying to build the NFL's next great team. They hired Bill Walsh as their head coach in 1979. That same year, Walsh drafted a skinny quarterback named Joe Montana. Walsh believed that the 49ers could win games with short, precise passes. Montana was a master of this strategy. After the 1981 season, the 49ers met the Cowboys in a battle for the NFC crown.

The game was a thrilling battle from the opening kickoff. Every time the 49ers took the lead, the Cowboys answered with a score of their own. Midway through the fourth quarter, Dallas was ahead 27–21. It was time for Montana to go to work. Starting with the ball on his own 11-yard line, Montana guided the 49ers down the field.

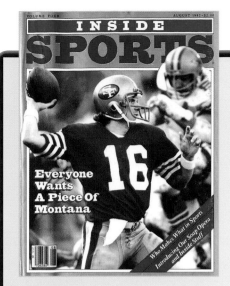

1982 Joe Montana
Inside Sports cover

JOE MONTANA

Montana was called Joe Cool because he was so calm in pressure situations. During his Hall of Fame career, he led his team to thirty-one fourth-quarter comebacks. Montana was named the MVP in Super Bowl XVI, Super Bowl XIX, and Super Bowl XXIV.

DWIGHT CLARK

Clark was Montana's favorite receiver during the early 1980s. Clark was a great target near the end zone. He caught 48 touchdown passes during his nine years with the 49ers.

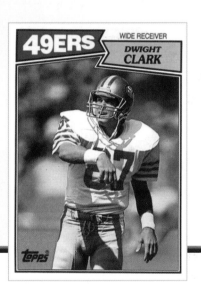

1987 Topps Dwight Clark card

With one minute to go, the 49ers had advanced the ball to the Dallas 6-yard line. Montana dropped back to pass. When he saw no one open, he scrambled to his right. Dwight Clark saw his quarterback in trouble and ran to an open spot in the back of the end zone. Montana knew exactly where to find him—the two friends had practiced this very play time and time again.

Montana floated a soft spiral. Clark leaped high in the air to snatch it. The 49ers won 28–27. This play soon became known as "the Catch." It dethroned the Cowboys and marked the beginning of a new dynasty for the 49ers.

RIGGINS RUMBLES OVER THE DOLPHINS

JANUARY 13, 1983 • PASADENA, CALIFORNIA

The NFL made headlines in the fall of 1982, but not for a good reason. Stadiums around the league fell silent for seven weeks. A labor dispute between the teams and their players shut football down. When the games began again, the Washington Redskins looked like the team to beat. They went 8–1 and were NFC champions in the shortened season.

Under head coach Joe Gibbs, the Redskins had learned to win the battle at the line of scrimmage, where the offensive and defensive linemen crash into one another on every play. The team that controls these battles usually has the best chance to win. Washington's linemen were nicknamed the Hogs. The only thing they loved better than getting dirty was blasting holes for big running back John Riggins.

The Dolphins watch from the sideline as John Riggins rumbles for his 43-yard touchdown in Super Bowl XVII.

The Redskins faced the Miami Dolphins in Super Bowl XVII. The Dolphins had an excellent team, but they usually struggled against big, strong blockers like the Hogs. Washington fans began to worry when the Redskins trailed the Dolphins 17–13 in the fourth quarter. The Redskins moved the ball across midfield, but their drive stalled. The team faced fourth down on the 43-yard line. Washington needed a few inches to make a first down. Gibbs called a running play for Riggins.

Washington quarterback Joe Theismann took the snap, whirled around, and tucked the ball into Riggins's gut. Riggins found an opening and pounded through for the first down. He then ran over Miami's Don McNeal, cut toward the sideline, and outraced the rest of the Dolphins to the end zone.

With one amazing run, the Redskins had turned defeat into victory. They scored again to win 27–17. Riggins set new Super Bowl records with thirty-eight carries for 166 yards and was named the game's MVP. He knew, however, that Gibbs and the Hogs deserved just as much credit.

COLLECTOR'S CORNER

JOHN RIGGINS

Riggins rushed for more than 1,000 yards four times with the Redskins. His greatest year came the season after Super Bowl VXII, when he ran for 1,347 yards and 24 touchdowns.

1978 Topps John Riggins card

JOE GIBBS

Gibbs won three championships as an NFL coach. He led the Redskins to victory in Super Bowl XXII and Super Bowl XXVI. He retired from football to become a NASCAR team owner but returned to coach the Redskins again in 2004.

1991 Pro Set Joe Gibbs card

FLUTIE'S PRAYERS ARE ANSWERED AGAINST MIAMI

NOVEMBER 23, 1984 • MIAMI, FLORIDA

Each year college football's top player receives the Heisman Trophy. Often the winner is the flashiest player on one of the country's best teams. Sometimes, however, an underdog walks away with the Heisman. That was the case in 1984, when Doug Flutie of Boston College took home the trophy. Flutie didn't look like a typical quarterback. He stood 5'9" and could barely see over his own linemen. He made up for this with a strong right arm and a big heart.

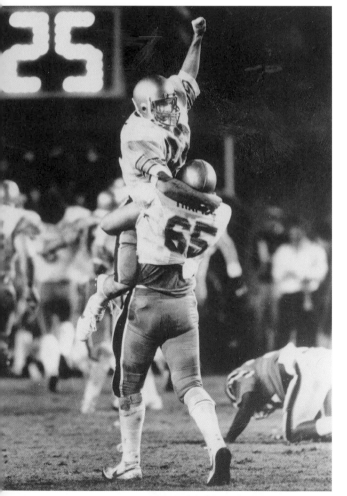

Flutie faced his greatest test on the Friday after Thanksgiving in 1984. He led the Eagles into battle against the University of Miami. The Hurricanes were a powerhouse. Their best player, Bernie Kosar, was already better than most NFL quarterbacks.

Flutie was not scared. Through the first three quarters, he matched Kosar touchdown for touchdown. With less than a minute left, however, the Hurricanes took a 45–41 lead. Flutie had one last chance to win—and only twenty-eight seconds in which to do it.

Boston College started with the ball on its own 20-yard line. Flutie completed two passes for 32 yards. The Eagles had time for one more play. They called a long pass known as a Hail Mary. It is

Doug Flutie jumps into the arms of a teammate after his Hail Mary pass to Gerard Phelan.

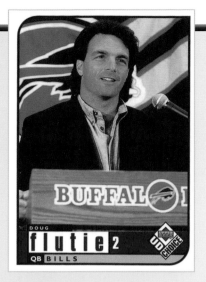

DOUG FLUTIE

Flutie finished the 1984 season with 3,454 passing yards and 27 touchdowns. He won the Heisman Trophy in a landslide vote.

1998 Doug Flutie Upper Deck Choice card

GERARD PHELAN

Phelan was a great friend of Flutie's and the quarterback's favorite receiver. In the win over Miami, he caught 11 passes for 226 yards.

Gerard Phelan autographed photo

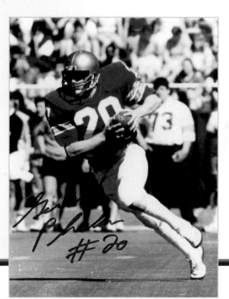

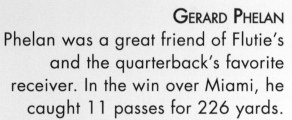

named after a prayer and for good reason. With the defensive team expecting a pass into the end zone, it takes a miracle for the play to work.

Flutie took the snap and ran toward his own goal line. He had to give his teammates time to reach the opposite end zone. He planted his feet on his own 37-yard line and heaved a high-arching spiral that soared through the nighttime sky.

Sixty yards away, Gerard Phelan ran behind the Miami defenders. He knew that Flutie could throw the ball over their heads, even from that distance. The pass came down through a maze of arms and helmets—and right into Phelan's arms for a touchdown. Boston College won 47–45.

THE "MUSIC CITY MIRACLE"

JANUARY 8, 2000 • MEMPHIS, TENNESSEE

NFL coaches spend months designing new plays to give their players an edge. They watch hours of game film each week. They study statistics until their eyes are tired. In spite of all of this planning, sometimes the best play is the simplest one—the kind of play that belongs in a backyard instead of an NFL stadium.

This was the case when the Tennessee Titans hosted the Buffalo Bills for a playoff game in 2000. The lead changed hands several times in this exciting contest. With sixteen seconds to play, Buffalo kicked a field goal to go ahead 16–15. The fans at Adelphia Coliseum in Memphis were heartbroken. They had come to see their Titans win. At this point, it seemed all but impossible.

A host of Tennessee blockers lead Kevin Dyson to the end zone for the Music City Miracle.

Tennessee head coach Steve Fisher had a trick up his sleeve. As his players took the field to receive Buffalo's kickoff, he called a play known as Home-Run Throwback. The kick bounced along the turf and into the arms of Tennessee's Lorenzo Neal. He moved toward the right sideline, where there was no room to run. Buffalo's tacklers rushed in for the kill. Neal turned and handed the ball to his teammate, Frank Wycheck. He was no faster than Neal, but he had a strong throwing arm.

As the Bills crowded to Wycheck's side of the field, he turned and fired a long, backward pass (called a lateral) across the field to Kevin Dyson. He was the fastest runner on the Titans.

With a small group of blockers leading the way, Dyson raced 75 yards for the winning touchdown. Memphis is nicknamed Music City. So naturally, the fans called this play the Music City Miracle.

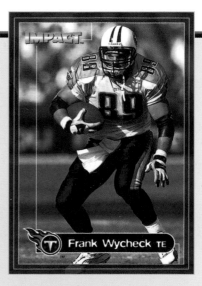

COLLECTOR'S CORNER

FRANK WYCHECK
Wycheck was a tight end who had his best seasons with the Titans. He was chosen to play in the Pro Bowl twice, in 1999 and 2000.

2000 Fleer Impact
Frank Wycheck card

KEVIN DYSON
Dyson was a good receiver whose career was cut short by injuries. He had his greatest season in 2001 with 54 catches and 7 touchdowns.

1998 Upper Deck Choice Kevin Dyson card

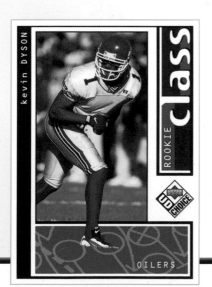

VINCE AND THE LONGHORNS HOOK THE TROJANS

JANUARY 4, 2006 • PASADENA, CALIFORNIA

College championship games are almost never as exciting as football fans hope they will be. One team usually gains an advantage in the first half and then wins the game easily in the second half. Many experts predicted the 2006 Rose Bowl would play out the same way. In fact, some thought the game would be decided before the bands performed at halftime.

The University of Southern California (USC) had a great team. The Trojans were led by Heisman Trophy winners Matt Leinart and Reggie Bush. USC's defense was almost as strong as its offense.

The University of Texas could not match up man-for-man with the Trojans. On paper, the Longhorns did not look as good. But on the field, Texas had one weapon for which there was no defense. His name was Vince Young. The Longhorns' quarterback was determined to prove the experts wrong.

Texas played well in the first half. After two quarters, the Longhorns led 16–10. USC came back in the second half. The Trojans took a 38–26 lead with less than seven minutes to play. Young needed two scores.

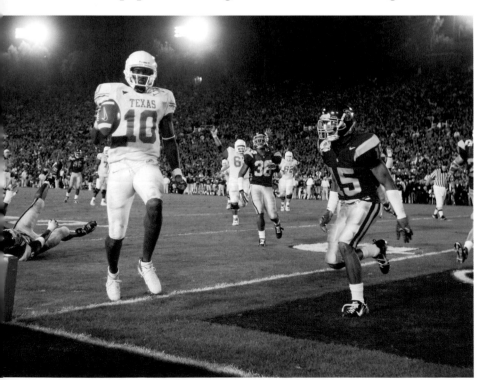

Vince Young crosses the goal line for the winning score in the 2006 Rose Bowl.

COLLECTOR'S CORNER

VINCE YOUNG

Young ran for 200 yards and passed for 267 yards in the Rose Bowl. He scored 3 touchdowns, plus a 2-point conversion. The following spring, Young was selected third in the NFL draft by the Tennessee Titans.

2006 SA•GE Hit
Vince Young card

REGGIE BUSH

Bush scored a touchdown in the Rose Bowl on an amazing run but finished with just 82 yards for the day. Bush was drafted just ahead of Young in 2006 by the New Orleans Saints.

2006 Press Pass Reggie Bush card

Starting on his own 31-yard line, Young passed for 44 yards and ran for 25 more. The final 17 yards came on a brilliant touchdown dash through the USC defense. That made the score 38–33.

With two minutes to play, Texas got the ball back for one final try. Young led the Longhorns to the 8-yard line. Texas faced fourth down. Young took the snap, exploded to his right, and won a footrace to the corner of the end zone. The touchdown put the Longhorns ahead 39–38. On the next play, Young crossed the goal line again for 2 points. The final score was 41–38.

3 DESTINATION END ZONE

THE ART OF THE TOUCHDOWN

No two touchdowns are exactly alike. The same is true of football's touchdown makers. In a close game, their talent, desire, and artistry with a football often make the difference between winning and losing. This chapter looks at the stars who have put their individual stamp on the touchdown. It shows how their special talents helped football become the sport that fans love today.

JIM THORPE

COLLEGE: 1907–1908, 1911–1912*   *PRO: 1915–1928*

*Thorpe played against other colleges and universities for the Carlisle Indian Industrial School.

At the 1912 Olympics in Sweden, Jim Thorpe won gold medals in the pentathlon and decathlon. King Gustav V proclaimed him to be the world's greatest athlete. Thorpe could do it all on the football field too. A powerful runner with explosive speed, he was nearly impossible to tackle. Thorpe waited for defenders to lunge at him, and then he would dart the opposite way and keep going. Thorpe was Native American. He learned football from the legendary Glenn "Pop" Warner, the coach at the Carlisle Indian Industrial School in Pennsylvania. Warner and Thorpe led tiny Carlisle to great victories over the top college teams. After Thorpe left the school, he helped make professional football popular. Most pro games at that time drew only a few hundred fans. When Thorpe played, several thousand would come. When the NFL began, he was both a star player and league president!

RED GRANGE

COLLEGE: 1923–1925   *PRO: 1925–1934*

Red Grange was known as the Galloping Ghost. Grange seemed to disappear as he

ran through crowds of tacklers, only to emerge on the other side. He was fast and elusive. Grange specialized in long touchdown runs. In his first game at the University of Illinois in 1923, he scored 3 touchdowns. A year later, against the University of Michigan, Grange stunned the Wolverines with 4 touchdowns in the game's first twelve minutes. He brought back the opening kickoff 95 yards for a score. He then added touchdown runs of 67, 56, and 44 yards. Grange finished his college career with 31 touchdowns in twenty games—9 of those scores went for more than 50 yards. In the winter of 1925, he went right from college

Red Grange (*left*) and Benny Friedman

to the NFL. After the season, Grange was the star of a long exhibition tour with the Chicago Bears. The team sold out each of the seventeen games.

BENNY FRIEDMAN

COLLEGE: 1924–1926   *PRO: 1927–1934*

During the 1920s, the football was nine inches fatter than the modern ball. That size made the ball very hard to throw. Normally, the job of the quarterback back then was to hand the ball to a teammate or run with it himself. Benny Friedman was football's first true passing quarterback. In his first game at Michigan, he threw 2 touchdown passes. Later in the season, he beat Indiana University with 5 scoring strikes. Friedman gained even greater fame when he joined the NFL in 1927. In each of his first four seasons, he led the league in touchdown passes. His record of 20 in 1929 stood for many years.

DON HUTSON

COLLEGE: 1932–1934   *PRO: 1935–1945*

By the mid-1930s, a new, slimmer football was being used in college and pro games. Passing, in turn, became a more important part of the sport. As quarterbacks improved their skills, their receivers became more important too. The game's first great pass catcher was Don Hutson (*left*). He was taller and stronger than many of the defenders who tried to cover him. Hutson was also faster and smarter. He invented many of the pass patterns receivers run today. In his second game with the Green Bay Packers, Hutson scored on an 83-yard touchdown pass. Soon he was being double-teamed and triple-teamed. This made little difference. By the time Hutson retired, he held almost every NFL receiving record, including most catches (488) and most touchdowns (99). His best season came in 1942 when he had 74 receptions for 1,211 yards and 17 touchdowns. That year Hutson won his second league Most Valuable Player (MVP) award.

SAMMY BAUGH

COLLEGE: 1934–1936   *PRO: 1937–1952*

Sammy Baugh made the touchdown pass into one of football's greatest weapons. Slingin' Sammy threw sidearm. Every pass seemed to hit his receiver right between the numbers. Baugh came into his own in the 1940s for the Washington Redskins. He led the NFL in passing four seasons in a row. While some teams would call pass plays only on third down—and almost never near the goal line—Baugh would strike at any time. He topped 20 touchdown passes in three different seasons and finished his career with 187. In 1947, in a game played on Sammy Baugh Day, he threw for 6 scores against the Chicago Cardinals.

HUGH McELHENNY

COLLEGE: 1949–1951   *PRO: 1952–1964*

No one ever told Hugh McElhenny that the shortest distance to the end zone is a straight line. Or maybe he never listened. McElhenny ran with long strides and pumped his knees high in the air. He could change direction quickly or spin away from tacklers. McElhenny was very hard to knock off his feet. Opponents often found themselves grasping at air—and then gasping for air—on McElhenny's wild, zigzag touchdown runs. Over his career, he averaged more than 7 yards every time he touched the ball. Nicknamed the King, McElhenny scored 70 touchdowns during his pro career. Many of those left fans—and opponents—shaking their heads in disbelief.

LENNY MOORE

COLLEGE: 1953–1955   *PRO: 1956–1967*

By the 1950s, football had become an exciting mix of passing and running. Players with sure hands and quick feet were asked to catch the ball and also run with it. Lenny Moore (*right*) was great at both. At 6'1" and 193 pounds, he was built like a running back.

But Moore also had the hands and speed of a receiver. Opposing teams were never sure how to stop him. Moore was a touchdown machine. During his twelve years with the Baltimore Colts, he reached the end zone 63 times on the ground and 48 times through the air.

JOHNNY UNITAS

COLLEGE: 1953–1955   *PRO: 1956–1973*

The player who helped Lenny Moore become a star was Baltimore's quarterback, Johnny Unitas. The NFL has never seen a tougher competitor or better leader. His first pass as a pro was intercepted and returned for a touchdown. After that, Unitas did all the scoring. At one point in his career, he threw a touchdown pass in forty-seven games in a row. Unitas worked hard during practice with his receivers. He wanted to perfect the timing of Baltimore's passing plays. That helped him to be at his best when the game was on the line. The Colts and their fans knew they always had a chance to win if Johnny U had the ball. Unitas retired with 40,239 passing yards and 290 touchdowns.

JIM BROWN

COLLEGE: 1954–1956   *PRO: 1957–1965*

Jim Brown (*left*) was one of the fastest men in football and also one of the biggest. He was larger than most NFL linebackers. It often took three or four linebackers to bring him down. In fact, Brown considered it a personal defeat if he was tackled by just one player! The Cleveland Browns' star was especially hard to stop near the goal line. In 118 games, Brown gained more than 15,000 yards and scored 126 touchdowns.

SUPERMEN

After many years of "war" during the early 1960s, the National Football League (NFL) and American Football League (AFL) agreed to work together. Owners from both leagues realized that there was a surplus of good players—and football-hungry fans. To draw more fans to pro football, the NFL and AFL agreed to create a new title game. The winner of the AFL would play the winner of the NFL for the world championship.

The leagues met to make plans for this big event. At first, everyone called it the AFL–NFL World Championship Game (*right*). That wasn't very catchy. The NFL commissioner wanted to call it the Big One. That didn't sound quite right, either.

One of the owners planning the game was Lamar Hunt. He ran the Kansas City Chiefs of the AFL. Hunt suggested the name Super Bowl. Everyone loved the idea. Only later did Hunt remember where he got the idea. His children had a new favorite toy called a Super Ball!

The leagues also talked about the best way to identify each Super Bowl. The game would be played a few weeks after the season ended, in January or February. That meant the 1980 Super Bowl, for example, would be the championship of the 1979 season. This would be too confusing to many fans.

In the end, Roman numerals were chosen to tell the games apart. At the time, the dates of movies were written out in Roman numerals. The NFL and AFL also knew that most children learned Roman numerals in school. Super Bowl I was played in January of 1967 between the Chiefs and Green Bay Packers. Hunt didn't think the game was super—Kansas City lost, 35–10.

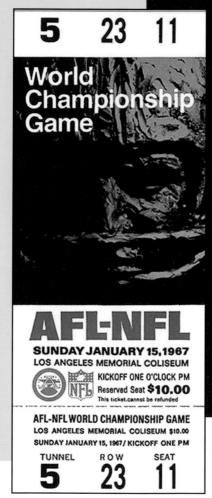

GALE SAYERS

COLLEGE: 1962–1964   *PRO: 1965–1971*

Gale Sayers was one of the most exciting players in football history. He was known as the "Kansas Comet." Sayers lived to break loose in the open field. When he found a little space, no one could catch him. In his first NFL preseason game, Sayers ran back a punt 77 yards for a touchdown. Next, he returned a kickoff 93 yards into the end zone. During the regular season, Sayers was even better. On a slippery, muddy field against the San Francisco 49ers in 1965, he tied a league record with 6 touchdowns. Sayers could stop and change direction so quickly that tacklers often missed him completely. Even after suffering a terrible knee injury, he was still one of the NFL's top runners.

KEN STABLER

COLLEGE: 1967–1969   *PRO: 1970–1984*

Ken Stabler was known as the Snake. This might seem like a strange nickname for a quarterback, but Stabler earned it by wriggling out of tight spots and making great plays. Stabler confounded opponents time and again, especially late in games. He could scramble out of the pocket for a big run or thread a pass to a teammate through a swarm of defenders. Oakland Raiders fans will always remember the touchdown pass Stabler threw to Clarence Davis to beat the Miami Dolphins in the 1974 NFL

playoffs. As he was being sacked, Stabler floated a wobbly spiral into the end zone that his running back caught between four defenders. It was one of many fantastic touchdowns the Snake produced.

WALTER PAYTON

COLLEGE: 1972–1974   *PRO: 1975–1987*

Walter Payton (*left*) of the Chicago Bears proved that a player does not have to look like Jim Brown to be a powerful runner. Known as Sweetness, Payton stood less than six feet tall and weighed only two hundred pounds, but he was a human battering ram. When Payton was being tackled, he liked to hit the defender first! Payton was impossible to stop near the goal line. He was strong enough to burst straight through the line. He was fast enough to outrace tacklers to the corner. Sometimes Payton fooled the defense by leaping over everyone and landing on the other side of the goal line. He ran for 110 touchdowns during his career.

MARCUS ALLEN

COLLEGE: 1978–1981   *PRO: 1982–1997*

Players who have a talent for scoring touchdowns are sometimes said to have "a nose for the end zone." This phrase described Marcus Allen. He first made headlines at USC when he won the Heisman Trophy in 1981. During one game that season, he rushed for 289 yards and 4 touchdowns. Allen joined the NFL the following year. He scored 16 touchdowns in just nine games during his first season. Allen amazed NFL fans with his touchdown runs. He led the Raiders to victory in Super Bowl XVIII and was named the NFL's MVP in 1985.

JOHN ELWAY

COLLEGE: 1979–1982   *PRO: 1983–1998*

Quarterbacks are often judged by how well they do with the clock winding down. No passer was better during these precious seconds than John Elway (*right*). The Denver Broncos' quarterback loved being on the field when the pressure was greatest. Elway threw the ball very hard. Usually his receiver was the only one who had a chance to catch it. If his teammates were covered, Elway would tuck the ball under his arm and tear down the field like a running back. That made him a nightmare to defend near the goal line. During his sixteen-year career, Elway threw for 300 touchdowns and ran for 33.

DAN MARINO

COLLEGE: 1979–1982   *PRO: 1983–1998*

During the 1980s, quarterbacks took center stage in the NFL. Many teams made the pass their top weapon. Most coaches believed that it took an experienced quarterback for this plan to work—until Dan Marino (*left*) came along. He was a star from the moment he stepped on the field for the Miami Dolphins. Marino launched his passes so quickly that teams did not know how to stop him. With one glance at the defense, Marino instantly knew which of his receivers would be open. In just his second season, he threw 48 touchdown passes. By the time Marino retired, he had thrown for 420.

JERRY RICE

COLLEGE: 1981–1984   *PRO: 1985–2004*

For many years, NFL coaches thought that the best way to score long touchdowns was a long pass to a speedy receiver. Jerry Rice showed you could turn short passes into long touchdowns after the catch. No one was better at grabbing a ball out of the air, making a quick move, and then outrunning opponents to the end zone. Rice was so good at this that the NFL had to create a new statistic: yards after catch (YAC). Rice set a record with 197 touchdown receptions during his twenty-season career. He also crossed the goal line ten times on running plays. In 1987 Rice scored 23 touchdowns in only twelve games.

DEION SANDERS

COLLEGE: 1985–1988   *PRO: 1989–2005*

The job of an NFL cornerback is to cover receivers and prevent long gains. Deion Sanders (*right*) believed he could do even more to help his team. Sanders had breakaway speed and the sure hands of a receiver. He would wait for a quarterback to make a mistake. When that happened, Sanders would intercept the ball with one thing on his mind: reaching the end zone. Sanders intercepted 53 passes in his career and returned 9 of them for touchdowns. He was just as dangerous on punts and kickoffs, with 9 touchdown returns.

EMMITT SMITH

COLLEGE: 1987–1990   *PRO: 1990–2004*

Great teams need a player who can "punch it in" at the end of a long drive. During the 1990s, Emmitt Smith did this job for the Dallas Cowboys. The team won three Super Bowls with Smith in the backfield. He stood only 5'9" but used his size to his advantage. Smith ran low to the ground and was hard for taller players to tackle. Near the goal line, he was like a bowling ball. Smith ran for 164 touchdowns during his fifteen-year career.

BRETT FAVRE

COLLEGE: 1987–1990   *PRO: 1991–PRESENT*

Brett Favre is what football fans call a gamer. He took pride in playing through injuries and personal tragedies that would have kept other players on the sidelines.

Favre was best known for throwing touchdown passes. Teams that played the Green Bay Packers—and later the New York Jets—knew exactly what Favre was going to do. Yet they still could not stop him. He believed he could complete any pass at any time. That made Favre one of the most exciting players ever to wear an NFL uniform. In 2007 he broke Dan Marino's career record for touchdown passes.

PEYTON MANNING

COLLEGE: 1994–1997   *PRO: 1998–PRESENT*

Modern football is a very complicated and specialized game. To play quarterback, a player's brain must work like a computer. Peyton Manning (*left*) of the Indianapolis Colts has become a master at this. Manning often walks to the line of scrimmage without knowing the exact play he will call. Once he sees how the defense is positioned, he barks out signals to his teammates. Manning's goal on the field is simple—he wants to lead the Colts to the end zone. It does not matter if they score on a pass or a running play. Even so, Manning is one of football's greatest touchdown passers. In 2004 he set a new record with 49 touchdown passes in one season.

TOM BRADY

COLLEGE: 1996–1999   *PRO: 2000–PRESENT*

A good quarterback uses the "tools" his team gives him. Tom Brady (*below*) does this as well as any passer in the NFL. When the New England Patriots have good runners, he relies on the rushing game. When they have good receivers, he passes. Mostly, Brady mixes his plays. This keeps opponents off balance and makes New England's offense tough to stop. Brady led the Patriots to victory in three Super Bowls in his first five seasons. Even so, most fans did not think of him as a touchdown maker. That changed in 2007, after a high-flying receiver named Randy Moss joined the Patriots. Brady broke Peyton Manning's NFL record by throwing for 50 touchdowns. Moss caught 23 of those scoring passes. This also set a new league record.

LaDAINIAN TOMLINSON

COLLEGE: 1997–2000   *PRO: 2001–PRESENT*

Watching LaDainian Tomlinson play is like watching a highlight film of every great NFL runner. He borrows something from all of them. Tomlinson has the speed to break any play for a touchdown, and he can overpower tacklers close to the goal line. Tomlinson is also a good pass catcher. In 2006 he set an NFL record with 31 touchdowns—28 on the ground and 3 through the air. Tomlinson also threw for 2 scores!

4 RUMBLES, FUMBLES, AND WRONG-WAY RUNS

FOOTBALL'S MOST REMARKABLE SCORING PLAYS

I f the history of football has shown us anything, it is that things do not always go as planned. Teams practice endlessly to perfect each play. Still, a slight misstep or bad bounce can result in disaster for one team and incredible luck for the other.

For example, fans of the Philadelphia Eagles will never forget how a ball bounced their way in 1978. And fans of the New York Giants will never forget either. There were twenty seconds left in a game between the two teams at Giants Stadium. New York had the ball and led Philadelphia 17–12. The Giants were ready to run one play and use up the rest of the time on the clock. If only it were that simple! New York quarterback Joe Pisarcik took the ball from his center and turned to hand off to Larry Csonka. But the pair botched the exchange. The ball dropped to the turf. Herman Edwards of the Eagles scooped up the fumble and raced 26 yards the other way for a touchdown. The amazing 19–17 victory will be forever known as the Miracle in the Meadowlands.

On the subject of amazing returns, nothing in football history was wilder than the play that ended a 1982 meeting between Stanford University and the University of California. After taking a 20–19 lead with four seconds left in the game, Stanford

The Eagles jump for joy as Herman Edwards completes the Miracle of the Meadowlands.

kicked off to Cal. Stanford intentionally squibbed the ball with a kick that skidded along the turf. The ball bounced into the hands of Kevin Moen. With nowhere to run, he pitched the ball to Richard Rodgers, who was quickly surrounded by Stanford tacklers. He then flipped the ball to Dwight Garner. He ran for 5 yards before tossing the pigskin back to Rodgers. Finding himself in the grasp of Stanford defenders, Rodgers pitched the ball to Mariet Ford. He sprinted nearly 30 yards before throwing the ball over his shoulder to Moen, the player who started the crazy play. Moen outran the rest of the Stanford players and crossed the goal line. Along the way, he bowled over a trombone player for the Stanford marching band—one of many people who had spilled onto the field thinking the game was over.

Sometimes, a touchdown occurs on such an odd play that it leads to a change in the rules. That happened with the "Holy Roller" in 1978. The Oakland Raiders were trailing the San Diego Chargers 20–14 with ten seconds to go. Quarterback Ken Stabler of the Raiders dropped back and looked for an open teammate. Everyone was covered. Stabler had no choice but to run toward the goal line. Suddenly the ball squirted free. Pete Banaszak tried to pick up Stabler's fumble and finish the play, but he could not control the bouncing ball. Banaszak batted it toward his teammate, Dave Casper, who was a few yards outside the end zone. Casper pushed

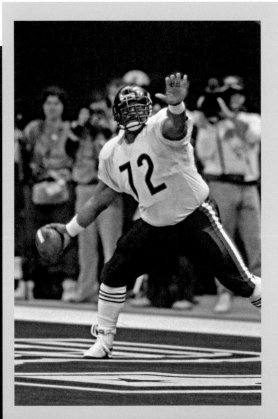

BIG AND SMALL

Touchdown makers come in all shapes and sizes. William "the Refrigerator" Perry (*left*) was a defensive lineman for the Chicago Bears in the 1980s. Perry stood a little over six feet tall and weighed more than 325 pounds. During the Fridge's rookie season in 1985, coach Mike Ditka put him in the backfield as a blocker on plays near the goal line. Tacklers would bounce off his huge frame, and the ballcarrier would score easily. Ditka soon realized that Perry might be even more dangerous with the ball in his hands. That season the Fridge rushed for two scores and also caught a touchdown pass.

On the other end of the size chart was Buddy Young. He was one of the first African American players in the NFL. Young stood only 5'4", but he was quick, powerful, and hard to tackle. At the University of Illinois, he tied Red Grange's team record for touchdowns in a season. Young played in the NFL during the 1950s. He often said that he faced more prejudice because of his height than his race.

and kicked the ball across the goal line, then fell on it for a touchdown. There was no rule against an "intentional" fumble, so the Raiders were awarded 6 points. They kicked the extra point for a 21–20 victory. The NFL quickly added a new rule to make sure this would never happen again.

Any time a team scores a touchdown on an unusual play, coaches work quickly to find a way to stop it. There was one play in the 1950s that no one could stop. It was called the alley-oop. The San Francisco 49ers used this play when they were near the goal line. Receiver R. C. Owens would run toward the back of the end zone after the ball was snapped. Owens was a former basketball star with great leaping ability. Quarterback Y. A. Tittle would lob a pass that only Owens could reach. As many as three defenders would surround Owens, but they could do nothing. If Tittle's pass was accurate, it was a touchdown every time. If he threw too high, it was simply an incomplete pass. The 49ers had everything to gain from the alley-oop and almost nothing to lose.

Sometimes a player scores a touchdown in his mind, only to discover that everyone else on the field (and in the stands) knows he has not. During the 1929 Rose Bowl, Roy Riegels of the University of California picked up a fumble and forgot which way to run. He was about to cross his own goal line when he was tackled by his own teammate! Had Riegels made it to the end zone, his team would have been penalized with a safety. Instead of scoring 6 points for Cal, he would have scored 2 points for the other team. Forever after, he was known as Wrong-Way Riegels.

In a 1964 NFL game, Jim Marshall of the Minnesota Vikings pounced on a fumble by the 49ers and took off in the wrong direction. Marshall actually made it into his own end zone, where he celebrated by tossing the ball toward the stands. He thought he had scored 6 for the Vikings until one of the 49ers thanked him for giving San Francisco 2 points. After the game, Marshall received calls from people all over the country trying to cheer him up. Among those who phoned him was Roy Riegels.

5 FABULOUS FEATS

AN INSIDE LOOK AT THE TOUCHDOWN

Touchdowns come in all shapes and sizes. Some are the result of trick plays. Others happen when good plays go bad. That is one of the fun things about football. On any given day—on any given play—either team can score.

History is filled with stories of trickery. Sid Luckman's game-winning play in the 1946 NFL Championship Game is a good example. Luckman was a great quarterback for the Chicago Bears in the 1940s. He was known as one of football's greatest passers. That December, Chicago faced the New York Giants for the league title. The Giants knew all about Luckman. Three years earlier, he had thrown 7 touchdown passes in one game against them.

Their meeting in 1946 was much closer. The score was tied 14–14 in the fourth quarter. Chicago had the ball late in the period. The Bears moved into New York territory. Head coach George Halas decided it was a perfect time to trick the Giants. He called for a "bootleg." Luckman would fake a handoff to a teammate, who would pretend to carry the ball to the right. All Chicago's blockers were to go with him. Luckman would then run all by himself to the left.

Chicago coach George Halas talks strategy with Sid Luckman.

Luckman took the snap and faked the handoff. The Bears were so convincing that every Giant started chasing the running back. Not until the running back had been tackled did they realize the ball was nowhere to be found. Luckman ran 19 yards into the end zone, and no one laid a hand on him. It was his one and only running play of the season!

The Miami Dolphins made an unforgettable trick play during the playoffs in 1981. The San Diego Chargers were beating the Dolphins 24–0, but Miami refused to quit. With time running out in the first half, they had the ball on San Diego's 40-yard line. Miami coach Don Shula told his team to run a hook and ladder. This play is named after the fire truck that has two steering wheels—one in the front and one in the back.

Don Strock fired a pass to Duriel Harris. Just as the Chargers were about to tackle Harris, he flipped the ball backward to his teammate, Tony Nathan. San Diego was caught completely off guard. Nathan made it easily into the end zone for a touchdown. Though the Chargers won 41–38, the hook and ladder gave the Dolphins the boost they needed to get back in the game.

Jerard Rabb dives for the game-tying touchdown in the 2007 Fiesta Bowl.

Boise State University took a page out of coach Shula's book during the 2007 Fiesta Bowl. The Cowboys trailed powerful Oklahoma University 35–28 late in the fourth quarter. With the ball at the 50-yard line, Boise State needed 18 yards for a first down. Coach Chris Peterson signaled for the team's hook and ladder play. Not only did the Cowboys gain enough yards for the first down, receiver Jerard Rabb took the pitch from teammate Drisan James and went all the way for a touchdown. The game went into overtime tied at 35–35.

In the extra period, Boise State used another trick play to pull out the victory. After scoring a touchdown against Oklahoma, the Cowboys chose to go for a 2-point conversion to win the game. This time, they ran the Statue of Liberty play. Quarterback Jared Zabransky pretended that he was going to throw a pass to his right but actually handed the ball off behind his back to Ian Johnson. The Boise State halfback trotted into the end zone to give his team a thrilling 43–42 victory.

The element of surprise is an important weapon in football. Devin Hester of the Bears proved this in a 2006 game against the Giants. When New York lined up for a long field goal attempt, Hester retreated to his own end zone. He wanted to catch the kick if it was short. The field goal was short. Hester caught the ball and started running. He caught the Giants by surprise. By the time they realized what was happening, it was too late. Hester sprinted down the right sideline for an incredible, record-tying 108-yard touchdown.

Whose record did Hester match? It belonged to his teammate, Nathan Vasher. Vasher returned an interception the same distance in 2005 against the San Francisco 49ers. Ellis Hobbs of the New England Patriots tied Vasher's and Hester's record in 2007. He did it on a kickoff against the New York Jets.

Amazingly, neither Hobbs, Vasher, nor Hester share the record anymore. Antontio Cromartie of the Chargers beat them all with a 109-yard touchdown against the Minnesota Vikings. On the final play of the first half in a 2007 game,

Antonio Cromartie celebrates as he scores his 109-yard touchdown against the Vikings.

the Vikings attempted a field goal. Like Hester, Cromartie retreated to his end zone to catch the kick if it fell short. He corralled the ball with little room to spare and then took off down the field. No one on Minnesota's team could bring Cromartie down. The record for the longest touchdown was his—until Ed Reed of the Baltimore Ravens tied the mark. In 2008, Reed intercepted a pass nine yards deep in the end zone and then weaved his way down the field for a score.

Reed, Cromartie, Hester, Vasher, and Hobbs all followed in the footsteps of Hobey Baker. He was football's first great kick-return specialist. Baker played at Princeton University from 1910 to 1913. He was a gifted athlete with dazzling

HE DIDN'T DO IT ON PORPOISE!

The most famous return of a missed field goal actually is listed in the record books as an interception. It happened near the end of Super Bowl VII. The Miami Dolphins led the Washington Redskins 14–0. The Dolphins decided to try a 51-yard field goal and sent kicker Garo Yepremian (*below*) onto the field.

Yepremian was a small man with a big leg. He had grown up playing soccer. He probably wished he had played a little more football when the ball squirted out of his holder's hands. Suddenly it was his problem.

Yepremian's first instinct was to kick the bouncing ball. He missed it completely. Next, he picked it up. When Yepremian saw a bunch of angry Redksins charging toward him, he did what almost anyone else would have done. He got rid of the ball as quickly as possible. The problem was that Yepremian had never thrown a pass in his life. His arm went forward, but the ball popped straight in the air and into the hands of Mike Bass of the Redskins. He ran 49 yards for a touchdown.

The Dolphins held on to win 14–7. Needless to say, the happiest man in the stadium—and also the most embarrassed—was Yepremian.

speed and quick moves. Baker thrilled Princeton fans with his daring running style, especially on punt returns. He would time his catches so that he got the ball while running forward at full speed. As Baker dashed toward the approaching tacklers, the excited crowd would shout, "Here he comes!" And often there he went. Stories of Baker's touchdowns are still told almost a century later.

Another famous return man was Jack Christiansen of the Detroit Lions. He used his blazing speed to cover the NFL's top pass receivers in the 1950s. He also had a special talent for running back punts. Christiansen returned four punts for touchdowns as a rookie in 1951. He was so difficult to tackle that every team in the league soon changed their punt coverage plays. Christiansen scored eight touchdowns on punt returns. He also intercepted 42 passes—including 3 he brought back for touchdowns. All these years later, Christiansen's impact on the NFL can still be seen. Teams continue to spread their players across the field when covering a punt.

FOR THE RECORD 6

FOOTBALL'S GREATEST SCORING MARKS

For anyone who plays football, putting on the pads and strapping on a helmet is a special thrill. Scoring a touchdown is an even greater feeling—especially if you do it in the NFL. The records set by NFL players are among the most respected in all of sports. To reach any of these marks, you have to possess equal parts of talent, timing, and tenacity. As of the 2008 season, these were the NFL's top touchdown makers. Of course, records are made to be broken!

MOST TDs

MOST RUSHING TDS

In a Game	6	Ernie Nevers	1929
In a Season	28	LaDainian Tomlinson	2006
In a Career	164	Emmitt Smith (*right*)	1990–2004

MOST PASSING TDS

In a Game	7	Sid Luckman	1943
		Adrian Burk	1954
		George Blanda	1961
		Y. A. Tittle	1962
		Joe Kapp	1969
In a Season	50	Tom Brady	2007
In a Career	464	Brett Favre (*top left*)	1991–2008

MOST RECEIVING TDS

In a Game	5	Bob Shaw	1950
		Kellen Winslow	1981
		Jerry Rice	1990
In a Season	23	Randy Moss	2007
In a Career	197	Jerry Rice	1985–2004

MOST PUNT RETURN TDS

In a Season	4	Jack Christiansen	1951
		Rick Upchurch	1976
		Devin Hester	2007
In a Career	10	Eric Metcalf	1989–2002

MOST KICKOFF RETURN TDS

In a Season	4	Travis Williams	1967
		Cecil Turner	1970
In a Career	6	Ollie Matson	1952 & 1954–1964
		Gale Sayers (*bottom left*)	1965–1971
		Travis Williams	1967–1971
		Mel Gray	1986–1997
		Dante Hall	2000–2007

MOST INTERCEPTION RETURN TDS

In a Season	4	Ken Houston	1971
		Jim Kearney	1972
		Eric Allen	1993
In a Career	12	Rod Woodson	1987–2003

LONGEST TDs

LONGEST TDS

Rushing	99 yards	Tony Dorsett (*right*)	1983
Passing	99 yards	Frank Filchock to Andy Farkas	1939
		George Izo to Bobby Mitchell	1963
		Karl Sweetan to Pat Studstill	1966
		Sonny Jurgensen to Gerry Allen	1968
		Jim Plunkett to Cliff Branch	1983
		Ron Jaworski to Mike Quick	1985
		Stan Humphries to Tony Martin	1994
		Brett Favre to Robert Brooks	1995
		Trent Green to Marc Boerigter	2002
		Jeff Garcia to Andre Davis	2004
		Gus Frerotte to Bernard Berrian	2008
Punt Return	103 yards	Robert Bailey	1994
Kickoff Return	108 yards	Ellis Hobbs (*below*)	2007
Interception Return	108 yards	Ed Reed	2008

SUPER BOWL TDs

MOST RUSHING TDS

In a Game	3	Terrell Davis
In a Career	5	Emmitt Smith
Longest	75 yards	Willie Parker

MOST PASSING TDS

In a Game	6	Steve Young
In a Career	11	Joe Montana (*top left*)
Longest	85 yards	Jake Delhomme

MOST RECEIVING TDS

In a Game	3	Jerry Rice (twice)
In a Career	8	Jerry Rice
Longest	85 yards	Muhsin Muhammad

MOST INTERCEPTION RETURN TDS

In a Game	2	Dwight Smith
Longest	100 yards	James Harrison (*bottom left*)

MOST KICKOFF RETURN TDS

In a Game	1	Fulton Walker
		Stanford Jennings
		Andre Coleman
		Desmond Howard
		Tim Dwight
		Ron Dixon
		Jermaine Lewis
		Devin Hester
Longest	99 yards	Desmond Howard

CROSSING THE GOAL LINE 7

THE FUTURE OF THE TOUCHDOWN

Bigger, faster, smarter, and stronger—it is not hard to see the difference between today's stars and the players from the past. The first football players stood an average of only 5'6" and weighed 150 or 160 pounds. A muscular six-footer with some agility could dominate those early games.

Now that same six-footer must have world-class sprinting speed and a brain that scans the field like a computer just to make an NFL team. In fifty or one hundred years, it is safe to say that football players will be even bigger, faster, smarter, and stronger than they are now.

How will this change the game? From the standpoint of a fan, it may not change very much. In fact, from the stands, a football game may look the same to your future grandchildren as it does to you at this time. The field will have the same dimensions. There will still be eleven players on a side. The team with the ball will still be trying to make first downs and cross the goal line.

Most of the plays now used by high school, college, and pro teams will still be used in the future. The players represented by the Xs and Os will improve, but

Excited fans in San Diego are the picture of joy after a touchdown by LaDainian Tomlinson.

they will improve in relation to one another. So the basics of football are unlikely to undergo a major change.

What will the main differences be? Blocks will happen a split second faster. Collisions between players will have more energy. Passes may travel a few feet farther and faster. Kicked balls may fly a little straighter. One thing that will not be different is the hunger of players to reach the end zone—neither will the determination of the players who are trying to stop them.

This is great news for football fans. It guarantees that the touchdown will remain one of the most thrilling plays in sports … and that there will be many more talented and creative athletes giving everything they've got to cross the goal line.

RESOURCES

WEBSITES

Football Hall of Fame   **http://www.profootballhof.com**
The official site of the Football Hall of Fame features information on the greatest players in football history,
including their biographies and statistics.

JockBio   **http://www.jockbio.com**
The Web's most comprehensive biographical sports site features profiles of the top NFL players, plus a daily
list of their birthdays.

NCAA   **http://www.ncaa.com/sports/m-footbl/ncaa-m-footbl-body.html**
The official site of the National Collegiate Athletics Association features information on each division of
college football, including statistics and historical facts.

NFL   **http://www.nfl.com**
The official site of the National Football League features information on teams and players, plus statistics,
NFL history, and the official NFL rules.

BOOKS

Boyles, Bob, and Paul Guido. *50 Years of College Football: A Modern History of America's Most Colorful Sport.*
     New York: Skyhorse Publishing, 2007.

Buckman, Virginia. *Football Stars.* San Francisco: Children's Press, 2007.

Editors of Sports Illustrated. *The College Football Book.* New York: Sports Illustrated, 2008.

Fleder, Rob, ed. *The Football Book.* New York: Sports Illustrated, 2005.

Gay, Timothy. *The Physics of Football: Discover the Science of Bone-Crunching Hits, Soaring Field Goals, and
     Awe-Inspiring Passes.* New York: Harper Paperbacks, 2005.

Lahman, Sean. *The Pro Football Historical Abstract: A Hardcore Fan's Guide to All-Time Player Rankings.* Guilford,
     CT: Lyons Press, 2008.

Maki, Allan. *Football's Greatest Stars.* Ontario, Canada: Firefly Books, 2008.

Mehno, John. *The Best Book of Football Facts and Stats.* Ontario: Firefly Books, 2004.

Palmer, Peter, Ken Pullis, Sean Lahman, Tod Maher, Matthew Silverman, and Gary Gillette, eds. *The ESPN Pro
     Football Encyclopedia.* New York: Sterling Publishing, 2007.

INDEX

Page numbers in italics refer to illustrations.